Once Upon a Flying Fish is dedicated to my family. Without their love and support none of this would be possible.

HUGS!

Strauberry Studios Press
a division of strauberry studios

Once Upon a Flying Fish
Written and illustrated by Susan Straub-Martin

All photos, story, illustrations & characters are
© 2010 of Susan Straub-Martin All rights reserved.

No part of this publication may be reproduced or stored in a retrieval system or transmitted in any form or by any means, electronic, mechanical, photocopying, recording, or otherwise without written permission of publisher. Digital version available under different ISBN Number.

For information regarding permission, please write to:
Permissions Department,
StrauberryStudios Press
11000 NE 10th St. #230
Bellevue, WA 98004
Once Upon a Flying Fish.

Summary: A fun day out to the famous Pike Place Market. Friends Poppy Penguin, Frosty, Theo and Henri Bears meet at the market and have a fun day watching, playing, eating and of course getting into a bit of trouble. See all the sights and sounds of the market in this colorful fun adventure.

ISBN 978-0-9830321-0-6

(1. Fiction 2.Picture Book 3.Humorous Story)
Printed in the USA.

Illustrated using a variety of tools, Camera, Illustrator, photoshop, painter.

Once upon a flying fish

Written and Illustrated by Susan Straub-Martin

Pike Place Market is a public market overlooking the Elliott Bay waterfront in Seattle, Washington, United States. The Market opened August 17, 1907, and is one of the oldest continually operated public farmers' markets in the United States. It is a place of business for many small farmers, craftspeople and merchants. Named after the central street, Pike Place runs northwest from Pike Street to Virginia Street, and remains one of Seattle's most popular tourist destinations.
For more information
http://www.pikeplacemarket.com

© 2010 all photographs, watercolors and character illustrations,
Susan Straub-Martin. All Rights Reserved
www.strauberrystudios.com

Poppy Penguin wanted her bear friends from Brambleberry Hollow to enjoy one of her favorite places in the city, **Pike Place Market.**

Frosty, Theo and Henri hopped a bus at the edge of the North Woods and headed off to meet Poppy. They were to meet her at the base of the big sign next to Rachel the pig.

The bears hopped off of the bus and stood there for a minute smelling all the wonderful smells, and watched all the people running around.

At the bottom of the hill they saw Poppy and she was waving. "Over here guys!" She shouted over the crowd.

"Wow! What a fun place!" Frosty exclaimed as he found his feet dancing to the sounds of the music coming from the market.

They all watched as the fish mongers yelled and the fish flew.

"Throw one my way." Said Frosty The fish monger looked over and the voice was coming from a big polar bear.

"Let's go look at all the flowers", said Henri.
"Let's go look for some honey", said Theo.

"Oh yes, flowers, honey, fruits, fish, berries and all kinds of great things" Poppy explained.

"Where's Frosty? He was dancing to the music and now he is gone!"

"We have to stick together. It is a very big place. Let's go find Frosty." Poppy said worried about her missing friend.

The friends walked down a little ways and they saw Frosty. He found free samples of blueberries and his face and paws were covered in purple berry juice.

"Oh hey guys, I found the blueberries and they are really yummy!"

"Take your friend and find someone else's samples. He is eating all of my berries!" said the guy at the booth.

The friends walked down through the market Theo stopped.

"Hey guys, Honey! Isn't it funny they put honey in a straw. They have free samples, shall we taste!"

Theo dipped his paw into the jar of honey and friends followed along. Everyone laughed, but not the vendor.

"Just look at the mess you made! Go bother someone else!"

Happy and full the friends walked on.

"How beautiful are all flowers. Red roses, pink peonies, yellow tulips and orange daisies!"

"How very wonderful." Poppy said with joy, "Henri you could paint these."

"You are crushing my flowers!" said the vendor. Go away now and find someone else to bother.

Sticky from the berries and honey and covered in flower petals they were off again. As they reached the end of the market they saw beautiful paintings.

"How did you get to sell your paintings here?" Henri asked.

"Anyone can apply to sell at the Market." The friends started to laugh.

"Wonderful! Let's go back to the hollow and get Theo's honey, and Henri's paintings. Frosty can get a job with the flying fish, and I will sell flowers. We can all have jobs at the Market!" said Poppy with joy.

They hopped the bus back to Brambleberry Hollow laughing and planning the whole way home.

www.ingramcontent.com/pod-product-compliance
Lightning Source LLC
Chambersburg PA
CBHW060806090426
42736CB00002B/180